# Looking Good!

## How to Get Stylin' with Your Friends

For best friends everywhere

—J.H.

For my mom, who always looks good.

—T.M.

ISBN-13: 978-0-439-02013-8
ISBN-10: 0-439-02013-1

Text copyright © 2007 Scholastic Inc.
Illustrations copyright © 2007 Scholastic Inc.
All rights reserved. Published by Scholastic Inc.

12 11 10 9 8 7 6 5 4 3 2          7 8 9 10 11 12/0

Printed in the U.S.A.
First printing, September 2007

Friends **4** Ever

The New You!

# Looking Good!

## How to Get Stylin' with Your Friends

by Jo Hurley
Illustrated by Taia Morley

**Scholastic Inc.**
New York   Toronto   London   Auckland   Sydney
Mexico City   New Delhi   Hong Kong   Buenos Aires

# Rachel

**Name:** Rachel

**Nickname:** Red

**Pet:** Cat   **Hair:** Wavy

**Favorite Thing to Read:** Comic books

**Favorite Person at School:** Drama teacher

**Favorite Article of Clothing:** Peasant skirt

**Best Dream:** Win Academy Award

**Worst Nightmare:** Stage fright

# Sam

**Name:** Samantha

**Nickname:** Sam

**Pet:** Dog   **Hair:** Bangs

**Favorite Thing to Read:** Sports stats

**Favorite Person at School:** Coach

**Favorite Article of Clothing:** Jean jacket

**Best Dream:** Olympic champion

**Worst Nightmare:** Broken leg

# JESSIE

**Name:** Jessica

**Nickname:** Jessie

**Pet:** Turtle     **Hair:** Ponytail

**Favorite Thing to Read:** Anything!

**Favorite Person at School:** Librarian

**Favorite Article of Clothing:** Sweater set

**Best Dream:** Write a novel

**Worst Nightmare:** Computer crash

**Name:** Elizabeth

**Nickname:** Libby

**Pet:** Guinea pig     **Hair:** Curls

**Favorite Thing to Read:** Teen magazines

**Favorite Person at School:** All my BFFs

**Favorite Article of Clothing:** Can't pick just one!

**Best Dream:** Starting a new charity

**Worst Nightmare:** Bad hair day

# Libby

# What's *Your* Style?

Do you like to decorate (and redecorate) your bedroom?

WHAT'S A BETTER 'DO; UP OR DOWN?

Have you ever had a *serious* fashion emergency?

From your closet and locker to your mood and 'tude, individual style says a lot about the way you look at the world and the way the world looks back at you. Inside this book, we're going to lay it all out for you with groovy style tips, tricks, and multiple-choice tests. (They're easy, we promise!)

Follow Your ART

Reading Zone

Evaluate an old look...and dare to try a new one.

Share style ideas with your friends...and see what happens.

Before you can click the heels of your positively-pink pair of platform shoes, you'll be a style superstar.

Knowing your style is easy! Just pay attention to all the signs. . . .

My Way

SAM XING

# The Real Meaning of S-T-Y-L-E

Okay, I admit it. I'm not really into fashion magazines because let's face facts: Nobody *really* looks like that, do they? But that doesn't keep my friends and me from flipping through the pages for cool inspiration. After all, style is all about being inspired.

And what inspires my style the most is what's *inside* me, not what's outside.

A long time ago, my mom told me some important stuff about style that I never forget.

**1** **Appreciate** the things that make me special: the brown eyes, the funny freckles, the crooked toes—*all of it*. These are unique things that belong to me—and only me. Without them, I wouldn't be me!

**2** **Tell the critic inside me to just "Go away!"** Sometimes this grumbly voice in my head says I look ugly or messy. But I know that's not true.

**3** **Break the rules.** Don't feel a need to conform to the same style as everyone else. I don't need to wear the same style clothes or hang out at the same places after school as everyone else. I'm the only one who decides what style I have. Got it?

**4** **Keep it fun.** Style doesn't have to be so serious. Style is color. Style is music. Style is everything that makes a bold statement. Style should always lift you up—and never bring you down.

**5** **Accessorize—with attitude.** This is mom's favorite rule. She always tells me that personality shows style as much as anything else. "Hold your head high and speak up," she says. "Your attitude is your finest accessory." And so I always try to think positive and talk positive.

# What Does Ur Style Say About U?

I'd like to thank all my friends....

Most Athletic

Winning isn't everything— but it's a lot of fun!

Future Bestselling Author

YOU CAN NEVER BE TOO ~~COOL~~ SMART.

Ms. America 2015

Shopping, anyone?

## The Ultimate Stylist

Glue or tape
your photo here.

_____
Your name

## A Few Good Rules

Although style is all about breaking the rules, there are a few
guidelines you might want to keep in mind.

★ **Pay attention.** Style is all about the details. It's the lace trim on
your T-shirt, the paint color on your walls, and the way you giggle
when you tell a funny story.

★ **Make mistakes.** Style is trial and error. For every bad hair day,
you'll have a daring 'do that will make your friends stop and stare
in a *good* way. Experiment.

★ **Borrow good ideas.** Maybe there's some style solution you
haven't considered. When you see a cool look on a celebrity or
another kid at school...don't be afraid to make that look your own.

# Retro

Are you retro?

I love old movies.
Yes or No

I like to raid my mom's closet.
Yes or No

I like taking something old and making it new.
Yes or No

I'm a thrift shop shopper.
Yes or No

I like the faded, lived-in look.
Yes or No

If you answered Yes to at least three of these statements, you are!

## Retro-Active

**Fashion statement** . . . Something vintage

**In my hair** . . . Chunky barrettes

**On the dresser** . . . Lava lamp

**In my backpack** . . . Granola bar

**Favorite tunes** . . . Oldies

# Sporty

Are you sporty?

There's nothing like watching a close baseball game on TV.
Yes or No

I'm a team player.
Yes or No

Big dream: to win an Olympic gold medal.
Yes or No

Pants before skirts? Always.
Yes or No

I own a pair of cleats.
Yes or No

If you answered Yes to at least three of these statements, you are!

## Sport Stuff

**Fashion statement** . . . Pair of cross-trainers

**In my hair** . . . Ponytail holder

**On the dresser** . . . Soccer ball piggy bank

**In my backpack** . . . This year's lacrosse team schedule

**Favorite tunes** . . . Hip-hop

13

# Glam

Are you glam?

I think platforms are perfect.
Yes or No

I like painting my nails.
Yes or No

The more glitz and sparkle...the better.
Yes or No

Everyone needs a color-coordinated cell phone—and case.
Yes or No

Let's go shopping for a new party dress!
Yes or No

If you answered Yes to at least three
of these statements, you are!

## Wham! Glam!

**Fashion statement** . . .Dress-up

**In my hair** . . . Glitter

**On the dresser** . . . Jewelry box

**In my backpack** . . . Tween 'zines

**Favorite tunes** . . . Pop

# Mod-n-Funky

Are you mod-n-funky?

You can read all my T-shirts.
Yes or No

When in doubt, go for bling.
Yes or No

I need to know the latest trends.
Yes or No

Let's layer my clothes in cool combos.
Yes or No

I like taking risks.
Yes or No

If you answered Yes to at least three of these statements, you are!

## Mod Squad

**Fashion statement** . . . Belted T-shirt and jeans

**In my hair** . . . Butterfly bobby pins

**On the dresser** . . . iPod

**In my backpack** . . . Books

**Favorite tunes** . . . Alternative

# Girly

ARE YOU GIRLY?

Lace or taffeta? Both!
...... Yes or No ........

I think pink.
... Yes or No ....

I wear flip-flops with flowers.
...... Yes or No ........

Skirts only. No pants.
...... Yes or No ......

Girls will be girls.
...... Yes or No ......

If you answered Yes to at least three
of these statements, you are!

## Girl Power

**Fashion statement** . . . Layered skirt

**In my hair** . . . Bow headband

**On the dresser** . . . Pictures of my BFFs

**In my backpack** . . . My journal with postcards and pictures pasted inside

**Favorite tunes** . . . Girl bands

# What Not to Wear  by Sam

I love cracking a joke as much as the next person, but sometimes style and fashion are noooo laughing matter. I'm not trying to get all "mom" on you, but there are some things you might want to consider when you're examining your own style. Listen up.

Avoid animal products (if you can help it). Check labels to make sure they were not tested on animals. And think twice before wearing animal fur.

You don't really need makeup. Life isn't a Broadway show (sorry, Rachel!), so it's not necessary to wear purple eye shadow to school, right? Go for natural-looking lip gloss. They make it in all sorts of cool flavors (I love watermelon).

Check your *real* size. Try not to dress in too-tight tops or too-loose sweatpants. Shop with pals to find a wardrobe that fits just right.

## "School Uniforms Don't Have to Be Drab!"

Have to wear a plain blouse? Layer a colored shirt underneath for a hint of color.

Looking for a twist? Cinch a belt around your waist for a funky new look.

Feeling *blah*? Wear polka-dotted socks or striped stockings.

*Psst!* Before adding to or changing your school uniform look, check your school dress code. There are always some rules that are *not* meant to be broken.

# Who's a Better Trendsetter?

Are you cutting edge . . . or perfectly predictable? Are you a leader or a follower? Answer these quick questions to find out if your trendsetting style is more like Jessie, Rachel, Sam, or Libby.

**1** **You just got a new pet. What is it?**

    a) Bulldog

    b) Bullfrog

    c) Ferret

    d) Tropical fish

**2** **What picture is on the inside of your locker?**

    a) Your family at Thanksgiving dinner.

    b) Candid shot of you in the school play.

    c) Photo of you making a soccer goal last year.

    d) A torn-out magazine page featuring a boy band.

**3** What would no one expect to find inside your locker?

a) Gameboy

b) Copy of *Shy Girl's Guide to Life*

c) Dress

d) Sneakers

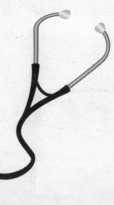

**4** Your idea of a cool birthday bash is...

a) Bowling with your best pals.

b) Having a costume party.

c) Shooting hoops and eating
   ice-cream cake.

d) Going to the hot new party
   place in town.

**5** What job interests you most on career day?

a) Journalist

b) Teacher

c) Doctor

d) Businesswoman

# So . . . who IS the better trendsetter?

If you picked mostly As . . . you're a TREND FOLLOWER—a lot like Jessie. You take things seriously, including the latest charts on what's hot and what's not. A big reader, you have big ideas about what you like to think/wear/say, but you usually keep those thoughts to yourself and follow the crowd.

If you picked mostly Bs . . . you're a TREND TWISTER—a lot like Rachel. You know what all the trends are, and you enjoy those trends, but you won't be caught dead looking, sounding, or acting like someone else! That's why you typically take something trendy and make it your very own.

If you picked mostly Cs . . . you're a TREND SNUBBER—a lot like Sam. You think trends are major dead ends—and you would much rather grab a soccer ball than stand around arguing which of you is cooler.

If you picked mostly Ds . . . you're a TRENDSETTER—a lot like Libby. You recognize when cool things are about to happen—and you seize the moment.

# Looking Good: Put a "Style" on Your Face

Remember: Style isn't just about what's in your closet or inside your purse. Sometimes you reveal a lot about your style when you reveal your mood.

Sad? A quiet frown lets people know that you're shutting down—and might need a bear hug.

Angry? A grimace and a stomped foot let everyone know: Stay away or else.

Happy? A great big grin tells the world you're friendly and approachable.

What kind of "style" are you wearing on your face right now?

SMILING IS HARD WORK. WE USE UP TO FIFTY-THREE DIFFERENT MUSCLES TO SMILE. BUT IT'S ALL WORTH IT. EVEN "PRETEND" SMILING RELEASES ENDORPHINS (CHEMICALS INSIDE OUR BODY) TO MAKE US FEEL GOOD.

Jessie Knows!

# Style Tip: Friendly Facial

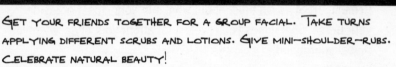

Get your friends together for a group facial. Take turns applying different scrubs and lotions. Give mini-shoulder-rubs. Celebrate natural beauty!

**· · · · · · · · · · · · · · · · · · · · · · · · · · You need: · · · · · · · · · · · · · · · · · · · · · · ·**

Large bath towels • Mood lighting (put a colored lightbulb into your bedroom lamp for special effect) • Hot towels (wet a hand towel and then microwave it for 30 seconds) • Pot of boiling water (add a drop of lavender oil or a few chamomile tea bags) • Simple face scrub, toner, and moisturizing creams • Soft music (environmental sounds can really chill you out)

## What to do:

1. Place your face over the pot of boiled water, but be very careful! You want to feel like you're in a steam bath but you should be at least 18 inches away from the hot pot.

2. Then place a large towel over your head so you are now inhaling the hot steam—and it's working its magic on your skin. The lavender or chamomile will relax you while you do this.

3. After a few minutes, step away from the pot and sit in a chair. Have a friend apply different toners and creams for the facial.

Have you been crying—or just staying up too late to study? Get rid of puffy eyes by placing cucumber slices on top of your lids. It really works!

# Totally Delish Lip Balm

Libby's Lip Balm

With only a few easy ingredients and a grown-up's help...you can make the yummiest lip balm ever. Look for the ingredients at your local health food store. Try making different flavors!

Safety Alert: Get an adult to help you make this easy recipe!

## You need:

5 tsp olive oil • 3 tsp beeswax • 1 tsp honey • 1/2 Vitamin E capsule • 6 drops of almond, peppermint, or lemon oil

## What to do:

1. Melt the beeswax, oil, and honey in the microwave or in a double boiler. You should ask an adult for help with this part since the liquid gets very, very hot.

2. After everything is melted, stir in the Vitamin E and scented/flavored oil of your choice.

3. When everything is blended, pour the mixture into a small container from the drugstore. After an hour, it should be cool and ready to apply.

When I made my lip balm, I added a smidge of Mom's lipstick to the melted mixture and it turned into my favorite color—deep pink!

# It's in the Bag

First decide which bag belongs to which friend. Then fill the bag with the correct three items by drawing a line from each item to the bag where it belongs.

Hobo bag

Backpack

Beaded purse

Duffel bag

Rachel

Sam

Jessie

Libby

Rachel—Hobo bag: theater flyer, paintbrush/paint jar, and microphone

Sam—Duffel bag: sneakers, baseball cap, and energy bar

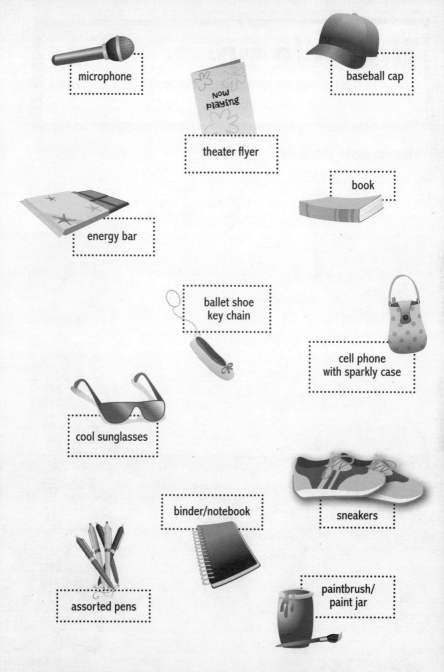

microphone

theater flyer

NOW playing

baseball cap

book

energy bar

ballet shoe key chain

cell phone with sparkly case

cool sunglasses

binder/notebook

sneakers

assorted pens

paintbrush/ paint jar

# Hair We Go

Nobody's stylin' unless she has a great 'do. Do you? Here are some of our best hair maintenance tips, so take note!

## Keep Hair Healthy

Trim your hair often to get rid of split ends.

Don't use too much gel or spray—
it weighs down your hair and makes it greasy.

Don't blow dry your hair every day —
that will make it dry.

# You've Got the Look

Blow-dry your hair upside down for a fuller look.

Change your part from one side to the other, or part it in the middle.

Go with a friend to a hair salon for a free consultation—and ideas for a new style.

Try a new shampoo or styling product.

Wind pipe cleaners in your hair when it is wet to create pin curls.

Don't just throw your hair back into a ponytail—curl it and wear it down.

Try a new kind of accessory, like chunky barrettes or wide headbands.

# Get Creative

When it comes to hair products, get creative. Mom complains when I want to buy fancy shampoo and hair gel. But I like the way the expensive shampoo looks in the package . . . don't you? Thankfully, I read somewhere in a magazine that I can save Mom money *and* have the cool-looking package, too. First I went to the drugstore to buy a small plastic bottle that's shaped like a fish. Then I bought an oversized bottle of shampoo on sale. I filled the new bottle with some of the less-expensive shampoo and PRESTO . . . *now* I've got the right stuff at the right price. I'm sooo much happier. So is my mom.

Having a bad hair day? Why stress out about your hairstyle when you don't have to? Take a dime-size squirt of hair gel and slick back your hair. Then put on a baseball cap—or any hat or bandanna.

## Style Swap

What are *your* favorite hair accessories? Next time you get together with friends, make a swap-and-trade hair salon. Everyone brings her favorite ribbons, bows, and headbands. Everyone should also bring her favorite shampoo, hairstyling product, and brush or comb. Take turns washing and blow-drying one another's hair like a real salon. Then give one another a new 'do.

# Rachel's Top Five List of Groovy Hair Accessories

**Barrettes.** You can get 'em with sparkles, jewels; in tortoiseshell, silver, or gold. They come in all shapes (triangles, rectangles, zigzags, and circles) and sizes (chunky, slim, and teeny-tiny).

**Stretchy headbands.** The brighter the colors, the better! They work equally well holding back curly, thick hair or fine, short hair. Sam wears these to exercise.

**Plastic or metal headbands.** You'll find this hair accessory in a lot of different widths and textures, too. Get a thick tortoiseshell headband for a cool, hip look. Use a pink-and-green, fabric-covered metal headband for a preppy look.

**Clips.** I always thought of those oversize hair clips as barrettes that grew teeth. These come in large sizes to hold back thick hair and small baby-clips to hold back a few strands up and down your head. I wear teeny, glittery ones when I dress up.

**Chopsticks.** One time for Libby's "Beauty Parlor" birthday party, we gave one another cool new 'dos. Sam and Jessie pulled my hair up into this big bun and held it together with pink plastic chopsticks—for real! I loved it.

# Cut It Out ✂

When real-life fashion designers design new clothing, they make "tear sheets" for their ideas. A tear sheet is like a collage of swatches (little strips of paper or fabric). You can make your own—with a little help from your friends.

**1** Grab a few old magazines. Flip through the pages without tearing anything out—yet. What images and words do you like best? Fold down the corners on those pages.

**2** Go back and rip out all the pictures you like the best. Snip the images or words with scissors *or* rip with your fingers. (Hint: Ripping may be better since this is a *tear* sheet you're making . . . LOL!)

**3** If your magazines don't have everything you want, look elsewhere for images: old postcards, newspapers, or your own photo albums. Find tear sheet inspiration almost anywhere. Print out a picture you see online or attach a paint chip or fabric patch. There are no rules about how much goes onto a tear sheet, so go crazy. . . .

**4** Once you've selected all of your items, apply them to a large piece of poster board. And don't be afraid to overlap!

**5** A tear sheet is art, so indulge your creativity. Once all of your images and/or words are pasted down, color in the blank spots with marker, trace images in glitter glue, or wash over the entire collage with watercolor paints. There's no limit to what you can do!

# What's Your Style Color?

## Take This Quiz and Find Out

**Which fruit are you?**

- a) Banana
- b) Watermelon
- c) Blueberries
- d) Grapes
- e) Fruit salad

**What kind of club would you and your friends create?**

- a) Ski club
- b) Shopping club
- c) Book club
- d) Drama club
- e) Scrapbooking club

**What is your favorite shape?**

- a) Circle
- b) Diamond
- c) Triangle
- d) Square
- e) Star

**Which lucky charm works best for you?**
- a) Rabbit's foot
- b) Unicorn
- c) Four-leaf clover
- d) Penny in shoes
- e) Anything with the number 7

**What would you choose as your theme song?**
- a) "We Will Rock You"
- b) "I Feel Pretty"
- c) "I Don't Like Mondays!"
- d) "If You're Happy and You Know It"
- e) "Somewhere Over the Rainbow"

**If you were a sweet treat, you'd be . . .**
- a) A chocolate energy bar.
- b) Strawberry shortcake.
- c) Ice cream with granola on top.
- d) Coconut cookies.
- e) Rainbow Popsicles.

**If you picked mostly As** . . .

you're YELLOW. You have a sunny disposition and a terrific laugh. Thankfully, you like telling jokes.

**If you picked mostly Bs** . . .

you're RED. You get angry sometimes...but mostly you're just pretty, bright, and out-of-sight.

**If you picked mostly Cs** . . .

you're BLUE. Boo-hoo? You get sad and serious sometimes, but you're always thoughtful. Friends love that.

**If you picked mostly Ds** . . .

you're GREEN and putting on a happy face is your #1 priority. You're the cheery one in a crowd.

**If you picked mostly Es** . . .

you're RAINBOW. Translation: you are a girl with a lot of possibilities. Sure, you can be moody sometimes, but who isn't? You don't mind mixing it up.

# When in Doubt . . .
# *Accessorize!*

**Baubles, Bows, and Other Beautiful Stuff**

I love wearing this oversize bead necklace that Grandma gave me for my tenth birthday. It goes with everything.

WHEN I WON THE JUNIOR CAMP TENNIS MATCH, I GOT A SPECIAL CHARM BRACELET AS A PRIZE. I NEVER TAKE IT OFF.

Mom always says my best accessory is my red hair. Even though I like having nice stuff, I still want to keep it real.

Does my faded blue hoodie count as my best accessory? It's ultra-comfy.

# Style Recycling 101

Why shop for new accessories when you may already own great ones?

**Idea #1:**

When's the last time you cleaned your room? Search your own drawers for hidden treasures. Something that goes out of style one year will probably come back into style at some point . . . like *right now!*

**Idea #2:**

Ask Mom or another grown-up if you can borrow something that belongs to them—like a cool belt or bag. Start a trend of your own.

**Idea #3:**

Trade styles with a best pal. Let your BFF roam in your closet one afternoon— and ask her if you can do the same. Search for the right add-on for your school dance party dress, or a hat that will look supercool for the class ice-skating trip. Borrowers, unite!

# Made in the Shade!

The best kind of accessory is the homemade kind. With simple tools like wire, beads, and a lot of imagination, you can make something very special for yourself—and your BFFs—in an instant.

## Instant Bangles

### What to Do:

1. Bend one end of the wire back onto itself. This will keep the beads from falling off the wire.
2. One by one, take the beads and slide them down the wire to the bend. Put the beads in any order you want. Keep same colors or shapes together or alternate colors and shapes—you decide what pattern you like best!
3. Once you've used up all of your beads, close off the open end of the wire by turning it back onto itself. This will keep your beads in place.
4. Now, take beaded wire and wrap it around your wrist as many times as you can. It should loop around a few times. Although it can bend, the wire will keep a firm shape. It should look like you're wearing a few bangles at once.

LOOKING FOR THE PERFECT BEADS OR FAKE JEWELS TO PUT ON YOUR WIRE? MAKE YOUR OWN BEADS WITH SOMETHING AS SIMPLE AS FLOUR AND WATER (SEE THE RECIPE ON THE NEXT PAGE). OR, GET BEADS FROM A CRAFT STORE. HAVE FUN!

# E-Z Dough Beads

···· You need: ····

3/4 c flour • 1/2 c salt • 1/2 c cornstarch • warm water

**What to do:**

1. Mix dry ingredients together.

2. Gradually add warm water until the mixture can be kneaded
   into shapes.

3. Make beads by rolling the dough into little balls, piercing the balls with
   toothpicks, and allowing the balls to dry. You can also string the beads
   through your wire (see above), letting them dry on the wire itself.

When the dough beads are dry, paint them different colors and designs!

# BEST in Shoe

What kind of shoe are you? Kick up your heels and take this short quiz to find out.

**1. Of the following activites...which do you do BEST?**

   a) Write thank-you notes.

   b) Play ping-pong.

   c) French braid my best
      friend's hair.

   d) Research my school
      science project.

**2. What is the BEST word to
   describe you?**

   a) Smart

   b) Fun

   c) Creative

   d) Steady

**3. What race car speed fits you the BEST?**

    a) Slow but sure.

    b) Leaving everyone in the dust.

    c) On the fast track.

    d) Middle of the pack.

**4. What is the BEST place to be after school?**

    a) In the library.

    b) On the playing field.

    c) My friend's house.

    d) Backstage

**5. What is the BEST food on your lunch tray today?**

    a) Vanilla yogurt with fruit.

    b) Tacos or pizza (I can't decide because I'm always hungry.)

    c) Salad

    d) Chocolate chip cookies

**If you picked mostly As . . .** you're a Mary Jane. You like

to be right and to do the right thing. Your parents taught you good manners! Mary Jane shoes are always girly, just like you, but practical, too. If shoes were graded on their smarts, you'd be an A+.

**If you picked mostly Bs . . .** you're a Sneaker. You're on

the go, go, GO! What's new? What's next? You ask a lot of questions and you like exercising your right to know stuff. Sneakers are great leaders *and* team players. You can take charge—but you're just as good at being flexible if someone else needs you.

**If you picked mostly Cs . . .** you're a Sandal. You're open-

minded and free-spirited. Your friends like hanging out with you. Sometimes you flip-flop (er, like the sandal), but you always manage to find your way.

**If you picked mostly Ds . . .** you're a Clog. You're

practical and dependable. You'd rather toil behind-the-scenes, but you deserve a standing ovation for all of your hard work. Bravo!

# Friend ~~Feng~~ Shui

Did you know that by moving certain objects around, you can attract more positive energy in your life? Just apply the ideas of feng shui (pronounced *fung shway*). Feng shui is the ancient art of keeping personal spaces (like your bedroom) in tune with the flow of nature.

FENG SHUI WAS FIRST USED IN ANCIENT CHINA, THOUSANDS OF YEARS AGO. IN MANY AREAS OF CHINA PEOPLE FACED GREAT FLOODS AND FIERCE MOUNTAIN WINDS. WHEN PEOPLE TRIED TO BUILD HOMES, THEY ALWAYS HAD TO CONSIDER THESE DIFFICULT WEATHER CONDITIONS. THE WORDS "FENG SHUI" LITERALLY TRANSLATED MEAN "WIND AND WATER."

**Jessie Knows!**

## It's All About the Chi

Chi (pronounced *chee*) is the energy that lives inside of you and inside of various objects in your life.

### Chi Fast Facts

- Mirrors, glass, and crystals catch and reflect sunlight, or energy.
- Wind chimes create a natural sound that is pleasing and energizing.
- Any lamps, but especially lava lamps, give off good energy.
- Plants and flowers symbolize life and positive energy, too.

# Our Best Feng Shui Tips Ever

De-clutter—now! I watch under my bed to make sure shoes and other junk like my lacrosse stick and shin guards don't get piled up there. No more mess! I think maybe I'll give some of the old stuff away to charity.

MY GRANDPARENTS GOT ME A ROTATING GLOBE THAT SITS ON MY DESK. IT HAS IMPROVED MY TEST SCORES—AND HELPED ME GET TO KNOW THE ENTIRE WORLD. LOVE THAT!

Mirrors bring good energy and light. It's also a great way to see a new haircut from every angle.

mom hung pegs on my wall to display my collection of vintage purses. She also framed a cute picture I drew in art class. It's important to surround yourself with personal, meaningful objects as art. Never hang anything dark or sad on the walls.

## Your Bagua Map

(Pronounced *bog wah*)

The map on the opposite page represents nine important zones for you. There are eight important building blocks of life plus one chi (at the center of the room). To improve good luck or success in any of these areas, all you need to do is increase chi in that area. For example, if you have a fight with your BFF, hang a crystal in your friendship zone to help make the situation better. Extra tip: Hang crystals on red cord. Red is the color of wealth and success.

## Feng Shui Tools:

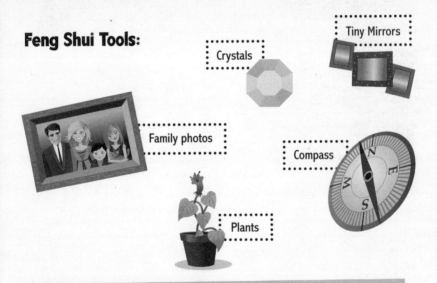

Crystals

Tiny Mirrors

Family photos

Compass

Plants

Find the entrance point to your room. (If there's more than one entrance, then stand at the door you use the most.) Now, use your compass to identify where north lies in your room. Facing north, you will see where the eight different areas fall in your room. Add a chi item to the area you want to improve.

# Your Room

1. Health *East*......................This area represents your body and mind.
2. Wealth *Southeast*...............This area represents money (like allowance).
3. Perception *South*...............This area represents how other people see you.
4. Friendship *Southwest*..........This area represents relationships in your life.
5. Creativity *West*....................This area represents your creative self.
6. Helpful People *Northwest* ...This area represents your body and mind.
7. Dreams *North* ..................This area represents your wishes for the future.
8. Knowledge *Northeast*..........This area represents school and learning.

## Some Feng Shui Bedroom DON'Ts

• Running water is good for increasing chi, but too much might disturb sleep.

• Don't put your fish tank in the bedroom; post pictures of fish or water instead.

• Don't put anything under your bed because it may lead to restless sleeping.

• Don't position your bed in line with the doorway. It is considered very bad luck.

• Don't hang a mirror directly over your bed. You don't want to get up in the middle of the night and be scared by your own reflection. In feng shui, mirrors are sometimes considered to keep the room "awake," which makes good sleep harder.

# Welcome to My . . . ★ ★ ★
# Fantasy Room

If you're anything like the Friends 4 Ever, then style shines brightest in your bedroom. It's your one personal space where anything goes. But as everyone knows, the only way to stay stylish is to make changes once in a while. Bedroom makeovers are a treat. With a few easy steps, you can turn a flowery room into a soccer stadium—or whatever you like! It's a perfect chance to make a fantasy come true.

## What kind of room suits you best? Name your favorites!

Favorite color :_____

Favorite texture: _____

Favorite piece of furniture:_____

Favorite picture/art:_____

Favorite fabric:_____

Favorite wall decoration: _____

Favorite place to sit: _____

# Think about different areas where you work, think, and play. Where do you . . .

Study? _____

Sleep? _____

Relax? _____

Play music? _____

Hang your clothes? _____

Talk on the phone? _____

Ask your best buds questions, too. What are their rooms like? Pretend you're on a television decorating show. Maybe you and a friend can swap ideas for redecorating.

Make wish lists of things you'd like to add or change about your bedroom. Tear out pictures from magazines with objects, patterns, or colors you'd like to use for yourself. Then save your allowance for a real room redo!

# Rachel's Funky Flowers

All my friends say I'm artsy, so I have a lot of art hanging on my walls. But there's really nothing tying it all together. I want a retro-looking room with bright colors—sort of like a cool garden.

## Hot Tip:

Whatever your room makeover, always be sure to have *original* art on your wall in addition to posters and mirrors. Frame a picture you did in first grade (and still love!). Or frame a collage of friend photos pasted onto a watercolor canvas. There are endless possibilities when it comes to homemade art. Try it!

## A Long, Long Time Ago

"When I was a little girl, the best part about my bedroom was my beat-up beanbag chair. It was sooo comfy. The only trouble was that our cat scratched it so many times that the stuffing came out. Dad had to throw it away. I cried for a week over that chair. I'm still sad. A chair like that would look groovy in a retro flower room." —Rachel

## Fantasy Room Must-Get List

1. Flower and vine stencils to paint along the borders of the room
2. Funky, patterned pillows in bright colors like sunny yellow, aqua green, or watermelon pink
3. Flower decals to stick on the walls
4. Shaggy carpet (green like grass!)
5. *Real* flowers like sunflowers or daisies in a chunky, funky vase

Get Mom or Dad's permission first!

### Do It

Paint your walls a flowery, fruity color—and then sponge paint on top of that. Or, paint each wall in your room a different shade of purple (or red or blue or whatever)—and then sponge paint different shades of pink on one of the walls.

*Fantasy Room*

# Sam's
# Good Sports

In a perfect world, I would have a room with a view of the ocean, ten pinball machines, and a fridge with an endless supply of sports drinks and chocolate ripple ice cream. Since that's way off the charts, I want any room with a cool sports theme.

### Hot Tip:

Make an ever-changing, "live" sports bulletin board. Get a corkboard that is at least 11 x 17 inches and hang it in an easily accessible area. Then make a collage with pictures of YOU in action: on the field hockey field, in the pool, or even at the stables. Because it's "live," you can change photos from competition to competition.

## A Long, Long Time Ago

"I really loved horses as a little kid. From my collection of ponies to riding lessons on weekends, I was sure that I would be a horse girl forever. Now, I still like horses but I'm more into sports." —Sam

## Fantasy Room Must-Get List

1. Posters of sports stars who inspire you
2. Trophy shelf (with a place to hang ribbons, too!)
3. Yoga mat for easy stretches and warm-ups
4. Curtains or bedding with a favorite sports team logo

Get Mom or Dad's permission first!

## Do It

Make a pennant display for your bedroom doorway!

1. Collect or make felt pennants of your favorite teams (you'll need 8–10).
2. Punch a hole in the upper corner of each pennant.
3. Run ribbon through the holes.
4. Hang ribbon along the length of a window or doorway.
5. Use small tacks to secure. Add buttons, patches, or tassels for more decoration.

# Jessie's
# Moon and Stars

EVERYONE SAYS I'M A BIG DREAMER, SO IT ONLY MAKES SENSE THAT MY DREAM ROOM HAS AN ENORMOUS MOON AND STARS AND OTHER THINGS THAT GLISTEN, RIGHT?

**Hot Tip:**

Stars and moons are popular decorative elements. You can find them on blankets, pillows, sheets, and rugs.

## A Long, Long Time Ago

"I'VE BEEN IN THE SAME ROOM SINCE I WAS A LITTLE GIRL. I THINK IT HAS BEEN PAINTED EVERY COLOR OF THE RAINBOW SINCE THEN. WHEN I WAS INTO SESAME STREET, I WANTED TO PAINT IT RED LIKE ELMO. WHEN I GOT A LITTLE OLDER, WE PAINTED IT PINK LIKE ANGELINA BALLERINA. I'M ALWAYS THINKING ABOUT THE NEXT ROOM MAKEOVER. . . ."

— JESSIE

## Fantasy Room Must-Get List

1. Midnight or sky blue paint for the ceiling

2. Glow-in-the-dark stars to affix to the bedroom ceiling

3. Chinese lantern hanging from ceiling for softer "moon" light

4. Star accessories like bookends with star cut-outs or picture frames painted with different-sized stars

5. Star quilt on your bed—with a large star in the center

Get Mom or Dad's Permission First!

## Do It

Paint one wall in your room with chalkboard paint. Then, get a bucket of colored chalk. Make your own art or write down messages for yourself with the chalk. You can change it every day if you want. . . .

# Libby's
# Glam-O-Rama

My ideal space is cool enough for a movie star with enough space for a dance studio. Mom calls my perfect style "shabby elegant" which totally sounds like something from a magazine, doesn't it?

### Hot Tip:

Black-and-white photographs look extra-hip in plain black or silver frames. Group a bunch of them together (different shapes and sizes) on one wall.

## A Long, Long Time Ago

"Growing up, I always wished I had one of those enormous closets like you see on TV, with a hundred pairs of shoes and clothes hanging everywhere and all the space in the world to get dressed like a movie star." —Libby

# Fantasy Room Must-Get List

1. Ruffled bed skirt
2. Lots of throw pillows for the top of your bed
3. Cute lamps for your bedside table—with an even
   cuter lampshade
4. Cover your chairs and tables in fabric
5. Oversize chest or trunk to hold all of your cherished dolls,
   stuffed animals, clothes, and more
6. Glam must-get: oversized mirror for lots of primping
   and posing

## Do It

Make yourself a glam throw-pillow cover with fabric paint and a lot of
imagination.

.................................... **You need:** ....................................

small to medium-size pillowcase or sham (in neutral color) • small paintbrushes
• 3 to 4 fabric paints • fabric glue • sequins, old buttons, fake jewels
• newspapers/paper towels for the mess

## Do this:

1. Lay out the newspapers on a table.
2. Select your favorite colors. Put one of your hands in the paint and then place
   your hand on the pillowcase to leave your handprint.
3. Make additional designs (curlicues, stars, loop-de-loops, or whatever!) with
   little paintbrushes.
4. Let the fabric dry flat overnight.
5. The next day, glue on the extra stuff, like sequins and more, and *voila!*
   The glam pillow has arrived. Just be sure to keep this away from the washing
   machine. Wash very gently by hand—inside out—and hang to dry.

# Style 911

by Libby

Having trouble figuring out your style?
Libby to the rescue!

## How can I have style when I share a room with my little sister?

There are a few things you can do. I'd split your room in half so she puts up whatever she wants on her side and you do the same on the other side. You can ask your mom to help put anything you may consider "babyish" in one area. The truth is that your younger sis might end up liking your style because it makes her feel older and wiser—and cooler. Be open-minded and share the space no matter what.

# I borrowed my friend's sweater and got a spot on it. Do I 'fess up?

You *have* to confess. Real friends don't lie or cover-up. If you hide it, you risk her never lending you anything again. Make it all better by washing the clothes or getting them dry-cleaned.

## I need to make a workspace for homework, but my room is teeny. Any ideas?

The best thing for you would be a desk area under a sleeping loft. You can climb up to sleep, and do your homework underneath. You could also create a "study chest" at the end of your bed. Get a plain camp trunk. Inside, keep your notebooks, pens, or even your laptop computer. Everything stays out of sight until it's homework time. Then you can sit on the floor, take everything out, and use the trunk like a desk.

## As if shopping with Mom wasn't embarrassing enough, she made a scene while buying underwear—and everyone stared!

Don't worry. My mom did that, too, and I turned five shades of red. I think it's my mother's job to embarrass me sometimes. But I know, deep down, she only says or does things because she loves me. She still lets me find my own style, and that's what matters most.

# How can I tell my BFF that her outfit is not working without making her feel bad?

If you really don't like her clothes, but you know she does like them, why say anything? If you feel like she's making a big faux pas (which is French for major mistake), then you could tell her, but here's how: Tell her something positive *before* you say something negative. You don't want to hurt her feelings.

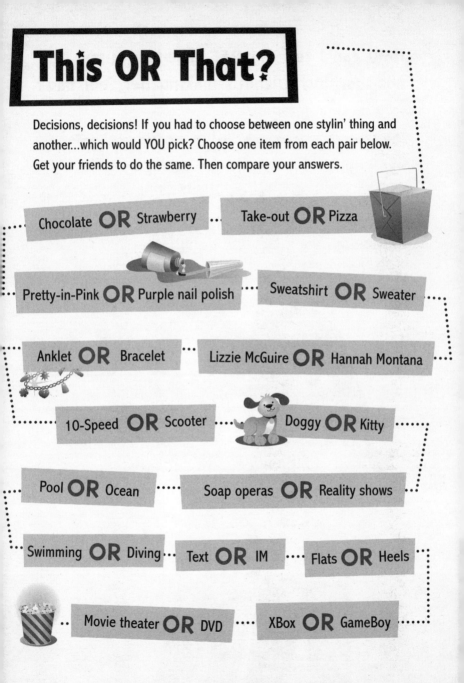

# This OR That?

Decisions, decisions! If you had to choose between one stylin' thing and another...which would YOU pick? Choose one item from each pair below. Get your friends to do the same. Then compare your answers.

Chocolate **OR** Strawberry

Take-out **OR** Pizza

Pretty-in-Pink **OR** Purple nail polish

Sweatshirt **OR** Sweater

Anklet **OR** Bracelet

Lizzie McGuire **OR** Hannah Montana

10-Speed **OR** Scooter

Doggy **OR** Kitty

Pool **OR** Ocean

Soap operas **OR** Reality shows

Swimming **OR** Diving

Text **OR** IM

Flats **OR** Heels

Movie theater **OR** DVD

XBox **OR** GameBoy

My whole life feels like a
soap opera sometimes.

I'll take the sandy
beach any day.

I'D RATHER COOK DINNER
WITH DAD THAN ORDER
TAKE-OUT FOOD.

I own a bike, scooter,
and skates. Rock on!

# Style Pep Rally

Give me an S!
Give me a T!
Give me a Y! L! E!

Two-four-six-eight, who do we appreciate? YOU!

Style shows in attitude. What are your feelings about yourself? Show off your self-esteem.

Don't let other people tell you how to dress or think. Just because it seems like everyone in school or on TV dresses alike or likes the same things doesn't mean that you have to like those things. Maybe you just have a different style.

Give me an L . . . for LAUGHTER. If you can't laugh at yourself, you'll lose your cool. You can get serious about style—but don't stay *too* serious.

Being healthy is always in style. Exercise, eat right, and get enough sleep.

Try, try, and try again. If you're focused and make your best effort, no matter what you do . . . that's true style!

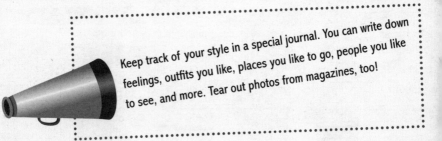

Keep track of your style in a special journal. You can write down feelings, outfits you like, places you like to go, people you like to see, and more. Tear out photos from magazines, too!

Get your best friends to motivate you! If you're feeling style-less, then get your pals to form a style committee to help you get motivated about your clothes, shoes, and more.

# Always Remember, Never 4-Get

Style is meant to be shared—and enjoyed.

The best style is the kind that may look fabulous on the outside, but that makes you feel good on the inside.

The most important person you're dressing up for . . . is YOU.

Try new things! Explore! Take risks! Figuring out your own style is half the fun